Nature's Guardian

Protecting Our Planet in Zoroastrian

Psalm Carnoustie

Tukotuku Publishing

"For all the young adventurers out there—may your hearts be brave, your minds curious, and your imaginations endless."

gies contained herein may not be suitable for your situation. You should consult with a professional when appropriate. Neither the publisher nor the author shall be liable for any loss of profit or any other commercial damages, including but not limited to special, incidental, consequential, personal, or other damages.

Book Cover by Tukotuku Publishing

Illustrations by Tukotuku Publishing

First edition 2025

Print ISBN: 978-1-991339-39-3

Ebook ISBN: 978-1-991339-40-9

TUKOTUKU PUBLISHING

Contents

Welcome to Zoroastrianland

The Big Bang and the Zoroastrian Twist

O nce upon a time, in a universe not too far away, there was a big, loud explosion called the Big Bang. It was like the ultimate cosmic party popper! With a giant "BOOM!", stars, planets, and tiny sparkly space dust began to twirl and dance. But here's where things get interesting—Zoroastrianism has its own creation story, and trust me, it's just as epic. Instead of a chaotic party popper, imagine a wise and powerful figure named Ahura Mazda showing up with a cosmic paintbrush and saying, "Let there be light!" And—snap!—just like that, the world was filled with mountains, rivers, trees, and adorable animals.

But every hero needs a challenge, right? Enter Angra Mainyu—the universe's grumpy troublemaker. Think of him like the villain who always spills juice on the fancy carpet. While Ahura Mazda was busy painting rainbows and planting flowers, Angra Mainyu was sneaking around trying to mess things up. But don't worry—goodness always shines brighter than mischief in Zoroastrianland!

In this magical world, fire isn't just for roasting marshmallows or making s'mores (though that is pretty awesome). In Zoroastrianism, fire is a sacred symbol—it represents truth, light, and the warm glow of kindness. Picture it like a superhero cape made of flames, always reminding us to be brave, honest, and a little sparkly on the inside.

Oh, and did I mention the festivals? Zoroastrian festivals are like the ultimate nature parties. Imagine giant picnics under the sun, bonfires under the stars, and everyone dancing like nobody's watching. These celebrations aren't just about having fun (though there's plenty of that); they're about saying "thank you" to nature for being so awesome and promising to take care of it.

But this book isn't just about history and cosmic explosions—it's about you! Yep, you, future guardian of nature and champion of kindness. Because here's the coolest part about Zoroastrianism: every good deed you do, no matter how small, helps keep the world balanced. Picking up a piece of trash? That's hero-level stuff. Helping a lost puppy find its way home? Instant superhero points!

So, dear reader, buckle up and get ready to explore Zoroastrianland. You'll meet wise prophets, cheeky animals, and maybe even a dancing flame or two. You'll learn stories about bravery, kindness, and the importance of respecting every leaf, drop of water, and little critter you come across.

By the end of this adventure, you won't just know about Zoroastrianism—you'll feel it, like a warm campfire glow in your heart. So, grab your imaginary superhero cape, pack some cosmic food, and let's dive into a world where light always triumphs over darkness, and every day is a chance to make the world a little brighter.

Ready? Let's go! Ahura Mazda is cheering you on already!

Ahura Mazda

The Superhero of Creation

Ahura Mazda is like the ultimate superhero of creation, zooming around the universe with a shiny cape made of light! Imagine a big, friendly face in the sky who loves everything that grows, sparkles, and wiggles. Ahura Mazda is not just any superhero; he's the creator of the world, and he made everything from the tiniest ants to the tallest mountains. He's got the coolest powers, like making sunshine and rain, and he uses them to help nature thrive. So, when you see a flower blooming or a butterfly fluttering, think of Ahura Mazda giving it a high-five!

Now, every superhero has a side-kick, right? Well, Ahura Mazda has some amazing helpers called the Amesha Spentas. These are like his superhero team, each one with a special job to keep the world safe and sound. For in-stance, one of them, named Vohu Manah, looks after all the animals and makes sure they're happy and healthy. So, when you see a puppy wagging its tail or a bird singing a cheerful tune, that's Vohu Manah doing his superhero thing! Together with Ahura Mazda, they make sure everything in nature is working in harmony, like a well-tuned orchestra.

Ahura Mazda loves fire! But not the scary kind that burns things down. Oh no! He loves the warm, cozy fire that brings people together. Fire is a symbol of truth and purity in Zoroastrianism, and it's like a magical light that helps us see the good in the world. Imagine sitting by a camp-fire, roasting marshmallows, and telling stories while the flames dance like little fairies. That's the kind of fire Ahura Mazda loves! It reminds us to be kind and re-spectful to nature, just like our su-perhero.

Zoroastrian festivals are like big birthday parties for nature, and Ahura Mazda is the guest of honor! During these celebrations, everyone comes together to sing, dance, and feast on delicious food. They thank Ahura Mazda for all the wonderful things he creat-ed. Picture a giant cake shaped

like a tree, with candles representing the sun and moon! Everyone is shouting, "Hooray for Ahura Mazda!" It's a time to celebrate
life, nature, and all the amazing
things that make our planet so
special.

As we learn about Ahura Mazda,
we also discover that being kind
to animals and nature is super
important. He teaches us to care
for every living thing, whether it's
a fluffy kitten or a towering oak
tree. Remember, every time you
help a friend or plant a flower,
you're becoming a superhero too,
just like Ahura Mazda! So, let's put

on our imaginary capes and join him in protecting our planet, because together, we can make the world a brighter, happier place!

The Great Battle of Good vs. Evil

In the land of ancient stories, where the sun shines bright and the rivers dance, there was a great battle between good and evil. Imagine a superhero clash, but instead of capes, there were flowing robes and shiny swords! On one side, we had Ahura Mazda, the wise creator who loved everything good, kind, and sparkly. On the other side was Angra Mainyu, the sneaky troublemaker who wanted to turn happy things into sour lemons. It was like a giant game of tug-of-war, but instead of a rope, they were pulling the hearts of people and animals!

Ahura Mazda had a team of friendly spirits called the Amesha Spentas. They were like the ultimate squad of nature's guardians. Each one looked after something special—like the trees, the animals, and even the sweet-smelling flowers! Picture them as nature's superheroes, wearing leafy capes and wielding magic wands that spread kindness and joy. They knew that every little creature mattered, from the tiniest ant to the biggest elephant, and they fought with love to keep everyone safe from Angra Mainyu's mischief.

Now, Angra Mainyu was not just a lazy villain; he was clever and tricky! He would try to make people forget about kindness and nature, like when you forget where you left your favorite toy. But Ahura Mazda and his team were always one step ahead.

They spread joy through festivals, where everyone would gather to celebrate life and nature! Imagine a giant picnic with music, dancing, and delicious food, where everyone shared stories of courage and kindness, while Angra Mainyu sulked in the corner, grumbling about how nobody wanted to play with him.

As the battle raged on, the animals became the true heroes. They knew the importance of teamwork, just like in a game of tag. When the birds sang sweet songs, it made everyone feel happy, and when the lions roared, they reminded everyone to be brave. Even the tiniest insects played their part, making sure flowers bloomed and fruits grew. Each animal knew that by sticking together and respecting nature, they could help Ahura Mazda win the battle against Angra Mainyu. Who knew that a little ladybug could be so powerful?

In the end, the great battle of good vs. evil teaches us an important lesson: by being kind to each other and taking care of our planet, we can all be nature's guardians. Just like Zoroaster showed us, every good deed, no matter how small, is like a spark of light that pushes back the shadows. So, whether it's planting a tree, sharing a smile, or helping a friend, remember you're part of this grand story! And who knows? Maybe one day, you'll become a superhero of kindness too!

Fire, Fire, Burning Bright

What's Cooking? The Importance of Fire

O nce upon a time, in a world before everything was so bright and shiny, there was just darkness and some very confused animals wandering around.

Imagine a lion trying to find his way in the dark! But wait! Then came the spark of fire, like a superhero cape billowing in the wind, ready to save the day. Fire became the ultimate flashlight for everyone in the Zoroastrian creation story. It lit up the night, cooked yummy food (bye-bye, raw carrots!), and even kept the scary shadows away. Talk about a multi-talented friend!

Now, let's chat about how fire is super important in Zoroastrianism. It's not just for roasting marshmallows, although that's a great bonus! Fire is a symbol of goodness and truth. Think of it as a magical glow that helps people see the right path. Whenever Zoroastrians gather for celebrations, they light up a fire, welcoming its warmth and brightness into their hearts. It's like a giant cozy campfire where everyone shares stories, laughs, and maybe even sings a silly song or two!

Have you ever thought about what fire smells like? It has that wonderful, toasty scent that makes everyone feel warm and fuzzy inside. In Zoroastrian festivals, fire isn't just for show; it's a special guest! It dances and flickers, reminding everyone that they should always be kind and do good deeds. Just like how fire needs air to keep burning bright, we need to be good to each other and our planet to keep the spirit of goodness alive. So, it's a team effort—kindness is the secret ingredient!

But wait, there's more! Fire also has a unique talent for story-telling. Picture this: a group of friends sitting around a fire, listening to tales of Zoroaster and other mighty figures. These stories are like adventures filled with bravery, friendship, and lots of funny moments. Each tale reminds us of the values of Zoroastrianism—like respect for nature and all its creatures. So, when you hear a crackling fire, it's like the fire is saying, "Hey kids, gather around! I've got some awesome stories to share!"

In the end, fire is not just about cooking or keeping warm; it's about bringing people together and reminding them of the importance of goodness and kindness. So, next time you see a flickering flame, remember that it's not just a fire; it's a beacon of love, laughter, and a little bit of magic. Just like the Zoroastrian faith, fire teaches us to shine brightly and protect our beautiful planet—one spark at a time!

Fire as Our Best Friend

A Zoroastrian Tale

O nce upon a time, in a land filled with magical creatures and sparkling rivers, there lived a very special friend named Fire. Now, Fire wasn't just any friend; he was the kind of buddy who could warm your toes on a chilly night and roast marshmallows like a pro! In Zoroastrianism, Fire is considered a super important friend. He's like a bright super-hero that helps keep the world safe and happy. Without Fire, imagine how boring it would be! Who would want to eat cold piz-za?

One sunny day, the wise prophet Zoroaster decided to throw a par-ty for all the animals and plants. But guess what? He needed Fire to help set the mood! He said, "Hey, Fire! Can you light up the sky and make some s'mores?" Fire was thrilled and jumped up and down, sending little sparks every-where. "I'd love to! But remember,

I also need to be careful, or I might get too hot to handle!" Fire was always a bit cheeky, reminding everyone that while he's a great friend, he can be a bit mischievous too. Zoroaster laughed and said, "Just don't roast the guests!"

As the party began, Fire danced happily, illuminating the world with his warm glow. He told tales of how he was born from the sun and loved to keep the earth cozy, just like a big blanket. The animals, from the tiniest ants to the biggest elephants, gathered around and listened with wide eyes. "Did you know," Fire exclaimed, "that I help plants grow by providing warmth? I'm like a magical gardener!" The plants swayed in agreement, and even the trees clapped their leaves in joy. They all knew that Fire was not just fun but also super helpful!

However, Zoroaster reminded everyone about being safe. "Fire is great, but we need to be respectful," he said, scratching his head. "If he gets too excited, he might throw a wild fire dance and start a forest party we didn't plan!" The animals giggled, imagining Fire wearing tiny party hats and dancing around, but they also understood the importance of being careful. Zoroaster encouraged them to always protect nature and keep Fire as their friend, not their foe. After all, having Fire around meant they could enjoy warm nights and tasty snacks!

As the party came to an end, Zoroaster and his friends made a promise. They decided to celebrate Fire every year with a special festival called Atash, where they would thank him for all the warmth, fun, and light he brought into their lives. Fire blushed a bright orange and flickered with joy, knowing he was loved. And so, whenever the kids saw a campfire or a cozy fireplace, they would remember the tale of Fire, their best friend, and how important it was to treat him with kindness and respect. After all, a little bit of fire can make life a whole lot brighter!

Dancing Flames and Happy Hearts

O nce upon a time in a world filled with magic and wonder, there was a bright and cheerful fire named Firoz. Firoz wasn't just any ordinary fire; he danced and twirled like a happy little ballerina! Every time the sun set and the stars came out, Firoz would light up the night, warming hearts and chasing away the darkness. The people in the land of Zoroastrianism loved Firoz because he reminded them of the good things in life: friendship, laughter, and yummy roasted marshmallows!

You see, in Zoroastrianism, fire is super special. It's not just for roasting marshmallows (though that's a big perk). Firoz represents the light of wisdom and truth. When people gathered around him, they shared stories about the world's creation, which was filled with talking animals, magical plants, and even a giant, friendly rock that told jokes! "Why did the rock break up with the mountain?" Firoz would crackle, "Because it felt stoned!" Everyone would giggle, and they'd feel the warmth of Firoz fill their hearts with joy.

During the festivals, Firoz turned into the star of the show! Everyone would decorate the area with colorful lights and dance around him. They sang songs about nature, animals, and the importance of protecting our planet. Firoz loved to hear these songs; he would flicker and sparkle, trying to join in. "I can't sing, but I can definitely glow!" he would say, making everyone laugh. The festivals were a time of happiness where everyone celebrated life, nature, and of course, how to keep the planet clean and green.

Firoz also loved to tell tales of great figures like Zoroaster, who taught everyone to be kind and respectful. "Did you know that Zoroaster once saved a deer from a tricky trap?" Firoz would say. "He didn't just save the deer; he invited it to join the feast!" The kids would clap their hands in excitement, imagining a feast with delicious foods and all the animals dancing in a circle, celebrating their friendship. They learned that animals were important in Zoroastrianism and that every creature deserves to be loved and protected.

As the night came to an end, Firoz would glow softly, reminding everyone to carry the light of kindness and respect in their hearts. "Remember," he'd whisper, "we all have a role in protecting our planet. Just like I light up the darkness, you can shine kindness wherever you go!" With that, the children would drift off to sleep, dreaming of dancing flames, happy hearts, and a world where every day was a celebration of life and nature.

Celebrate Like a Zoroastrian!

Festivals of Fun

Jumping into Joy

Have you ever seen a giant, fluffy cloud that looks like a marshmallow or a puppy? Well, in Zoroastrianism, the festivals are just as fun and colorful as those clouds! Imagine a day filled with laughter, dancing, and yummy treats. These festivals are like the birthday parties of nature, where everyone—yes, even the trees and flowers—gets invited to join in the celebration. So, buckle up, because we're about to take a wild ride into the joyous world of Zoroastrian festivals!

One of the coolest festivals is called Nowruz, which means "new day." It's like the New Year's celebration, but instead of confetti, there are blooming flowers everywhere! Everyone cleans their houses and gets ready to welcome spring, just like how a bear wakes up from a long nap.

People wear their best clothes, dance like nobody's watching, and feast on delicious food. Can you imagine eating sweet pastries while trying to balance on one leg? That's the spirit! It's a time to jump into joy and celebrate the beauty of nature coming back to life.

Another festival is called Jashn-e Sadeh, where people celebrate fire! Yes, you heard it right—fire! This festival is all about honoring the warmth and light that fire brings. Just think about it: without fire, we'd have to eat cold pizza! During Jashn-e Sadeh, everyone gathers around a big bonfire, singing songs and sharing stories. They jump over the flames (don't worry, it's safe!) to symbolize jumping over challenges. It's like a game of leapfrog but with a fiery twist. Remember to wear your superhero cape, because that's how you'll feel while jumping!

And then there's the festival of Ashoora, where people remember the amazing heroes and saints of Zoroastrianism. Imagine dressing up like your favorite superhero and going to a party to tell stories about all their great deeds! Kids gather to hear tales of bravery, kindness, and respect for nature. Just like your favorite cartoon characters, these heroes inspire everyone to protect the planet and be the best versions of themselves. So, grab your cape and get ready to be inspired!

Lastly, let's not forget about the animals! At these festivals, everyone remembers that animals are our friends and guardians of nature. Picture a parade with fluffy bunnies, majestic birds, and even a dancing goat (okay, maybe not the goat!). Zoroastrians believe in taking care of all creatures, big and small, just like how you would take care of your pet. Festivals are a time to show love to these furry pals, making sure they feel just as joyful as we do. So, let's hop into the fun and be the guardians of our planet, one festival at a time!

The Magic of Nowruz

A New Year Adventure

Nowruz is like the ultimate birthday party for the whole world! Every spring, when flowers start to bloom and the sun decides to come out of its winter hiding spot, Zoroastrians celebrate Nowruz, which means "New Day." It's a time when everyone gets together to dance, eat delicious food, and wear their fanciest clothes. Imagine a day where you get to jump around like a kangaroo, eat sweets that are tastier than a chocolate fountain, and make wishes that might just come true. That's what makes Nowruz so magical!

But wait, there's more! Nowruz is not just about the fun; it's also about nature and being kind to our planet. Zoroastrians believe that the earth is like a giant playground, filled with animals, trees, and rivers that all need our care. During Nowruz, families clean their homes to welcome the new year, just like how we clean our rooms before a big sleepover. This tradition shows that we should keep our surroundings neat and tidy, making the world a better place for everyone, including all the critters that live here.

Another cool thing about Nowruz is the Haft-Seen table. It's like a treasure hunt feast! Families set up a special table filled with seven items that start with the letter "S" in Persian, each representing something important, like health, wealth, and happiness. Picture a table with shiny apples that look like they could win a beauty contest, garlic that's good for you (and also keeps the vampires away!), and coins that jingle like a happy song. When everyone gathers around this magical table, it's a chance to share stories and laughter.

Nowruz also has a surprise element that keeps everyone on their toes. People dress up as animals or mythical creatures, turning the celebration into a fun parade! You might spot someone dressed as a lion, roaring joyfully, or a colorful fish that swims through the crowd. This reminds us of the importance of animals in Zoroastrian beliefs. They're not just pets; they are our friends and need our protection. So, during Nowruz, we celebrate not just people, but all the furry, feathery, and scaly beings that make our world lively.

At the end of the day, Nowruz is a reminder that every day is a chance for a new beginning, a bit like a superhero getting a brand-new cape! It teaches us to be kind, respect nature, and cherish the little things in life, like a bright flower peeking through the snow. So, whether you're twirling like a dervish or munching on sweets, remember that each moment can be filled with magic, especially during Nowruz!

Gahambars

Feasts for Every Season

Gahambars are like the coolest parties in Zoroastrianism, and guess what? They happen six times a year! Imagine a celebration where everyone brings their favorite food and dances around a giant fire! Each Gahambar is special because it connects to a different season and reminds us to appreciate all the amazing things nature gives us. So, get ready for some serious feasting and fun, because Gahambars are all about sharing, caring, and having a blast with friends and family!

The first Gahambar is for the creation of the world. Yes, you heard that right! It's like celebrating the big birthday of our planet. Imagine if the Earth had a party hat! During this Gahambar, everyone gathers to enjoy delicious food like bread, sweets, and fruits. It's a time to give thanks for all the trees, rivers, and mountains. We might even pretend to send gifts to the Earth! Just think of it as Earth's special day where we all join in to say, "Happy Birthday, Planet!"

Next up, we have the Gaham-bar that honors plants and food. This one is super important because it's a time to recognize the hard work of farmers. Picture a giant corn cob dancing to music while everyone munches on popcorn! This Gahambar tells us to be thankful for all the yummy things we eat. Everyone helps prepare a feast, and there's probably a contest to see who can make the biggest salad. So, if you love veggies, this is your time to shine!

Now, let's talk about the Gahambar of animals. Can you imagine a party where all the animals are invited? It's like a zoo came to life! This celebration reminds us to respect and protect our furry, feathery, and scaly friends. Everyone shares stories about their favorite animals and plays games like "Pin the Tail on the Donkey." We learn that being kind to animals is super important, just like being kind to our family and friends.

Finally, there's the Gahambar of fire, and let's be honest, who doesn't love a good campfire? This Gahambar is all about the warm and bright fire that represents goodness and truth. Everyone gathers around to tell stories, sing songs, and roast marshmallows. Just imagine sitting by a fire with your friends, sharing giggles, and maybe some silly ghost stories! This celebration teaches us to keep the fire of kindness burning in our hearts while we enjoy the magic of nature and each other. So, get ready to celebrate every Gahambar with joy and laughter!

Meet the Zoroastrian Superstars

Zoroaster

The Guy with the Great Ideas

Zoroaster was quite the guy! Imagine a friendly wizard with a big fluffy beard who loved to talk about good ideas and how to make the world a better place. He lived a long time ago, and just like a superhero, he had a mission: to teach people how to be kind and respectful to each other and to nature. He believed that there was a great battle going on between good and evil, and he wanted everyone to choose the side of goodness. So, he went around sharing his awesome ideas, kind of like a wise old owl but with a lot more pizzazz!

One of Zoroaster's greatest ideas was about fire. He thought fire was super special, like a bright, dancing friend that helps us see in the dark. In Zoroastrianism, fire isn't just for roasting marsh-mallows (though that sounds fun too!). It's a symbol of purity and truth. Zoroaster taught that when we respect fire, we re-spect the light of goodness in-side us. So, the next time you see a campfire crackling, remember that Zoroaster would want you to think of it as a little buddy cheer-ing you on to do good deeds!

Now, let's talk about celebra-tions! Zoroaster loved to party (who doesn't?) and he showed us how to celebrate life and nature through festivals. These festivals are like big birthday parties for the earth, where everyone comes together to have fun and appreciate all the amazing things nature gives us. Zoroastrians celebrate with colorful decorations, delicious food, and lots of dancing. If Zoroaster were around today, he'd probably be the one wearing the biggest hat and leading the conga line!

Zoroaster wasn't alone on his journey of great ideas. There were many other cool characters, like saints and wise people, who helped spread his message. Each of them had their own fun stories, kind of like superheroes in their own right. They taught lessons about kindness and caring for animals. Yes, animals! Zoroaster believed that all creatures, big and small, were important and deserved our protection. So, if you see a squirrel or a butterfly, give them a little wave because they're part of Zoroaster's big happy family!

Finally, Zoroaster helped us understand something super important: the choices we make shape our world. He shared stories about heaven and hell, but in a way that made sense to kids just like you! It's all about being good, helping others, and respecting nature. Just think of it like a game where you earn points for kindness and lose points for being mean. Zoroaster wanted everyone to play the game well and have lots of fun! So, when you think of Zoroaster, remember the guy with the great ideas who wanted us all to be nature's guardians!

Saint Stories

Heroes of Kindness

Once upon a time, in a land full of sunshine and friendly critters, there lived some really amazing people called saints. These saints were like superheroes, but instead of capes and tights, they wore simple robes and had hearts as big as elephants! They loved kindness and believed that helping others was the best way to make the world a happier place. They had some incredible stories that would make you giggle and cheer, just like your favorite cartoons!

One of our favorite saints was named Saint Khashayar. Now, Khashayar had a special talent: he could talk to animals! Imagine a saint who could have tea parties with squirrels and play hide-and-seek with foxes! One day, he found a sad little bird who had lost its way. Instead of just saying, "Good luck, little bird!" Khashayar decided to help. He climbed the tallest tree, flapped his arms, and made funny bird noises until the little bird found its family. That's right! Kindness can even help you make new friends, even if they have feathers!

Then, there was the story of Saint Roshan, who loved to plant trees. She believed that every tree was a home for a critter, and she wanted to make sure everyone had a cozy place to live. So, she planted a tree for every friend she had! When her friends asked, "Why are you planting so many trees?" she'd chuckle and say, "Because I want to throw the biggest party in the forest!" And guess what? She did! All the animals showed up, and they danced and sang under the shade of her beautiful trees. Celebrating nature is a lot more fun when you have friends!

Now, here's a funny twist: Saint Firoz had a pet dog named Zippy who was always getting into trouble. One day, Zippy dug up a garden where Firoz was trying to grow magical flowers. Instead of getting mad, Firoz chuckled and said, "Looks like you wanted to help me plant some new flowers, huh?" So, they ended up planting silly flowers that giggled when you tickled them! It taught everyone that sometimes, even when things go wrong, laughter and kindness can turn a mess into something wonderful!

In the land of Zoroastrianism, these saints show us that kindness is the best superpower of all. Just like how they helped animals and planted trees, we can all be heroes in our own way. So, whether you're sharing snacks with a friend, helping your parents at home, or even giving a smile to someone who looks sad, remember that being kind is the coolest thing you can do! And who knows, maybe one day you'll have

your very own saint story to tell,
full of laughter and kindness that
makes the world a brighter place!

Magical Tales of Zoroastrian Saints

In the land of ancient Persia, where the sun shone as bright as a shiny coin, lived some of the coolest saints you could ever imagine! These saints were like superheroes, but instead of capes, they wore robes and had magical powers that could make plants grow and animals dance. One such saint was the famous Saint Asha. Asha was a master gardener. With a flick of his wrist, he could turn a dry desert into a blooming garden filled with flowers that smelled so good, even the bees would buzz in delight! Kids would run around, laughing and playing hide-and-seek among the tall sunflowers, while Asha cheered them on, reminding them to always be kind to every little creature.

Then there was Saint Vohu Manah, who had a special connection with animals. Imagine a saint who could talk to dogs, cats, and even squirrels! Vohu Manah would have tea parties with the animals in the forest, serving them acorn cupcakes and honey tea. One day, a grumpy old bear stomped in, complaining that the forest was too noisy. Vohu Manah, with a twinkle in his eye, suggested they all sing a song together. And just like that, the bear found himself humming along with the birds. The moral of the story? Sometimes, a little music can turn even the grumpiest bear into a happy dancer!

Now, let's not forget about the magical fire! In Zoroastrianism, fire is super important, kind of like the secret ingredient in a yummy recipe. This fire isn't just for cooking marshmallows; it represents truth and light! Whenever the saints gathered around a fire, they would share stories that sparkled like the flames. One time, during a festival, they held a "Fire Dance" where everyone twirled around the flames, telling silly jokes and making funny faces. The fire would crackle with laughter, and even the stars in the sky seemed to giggle along.

As the Zoroastrian saints celebrated life, they also taught everyone to respect nature. For instance, Saint Khordad was known for his love of rivers and trees. One day, he saw some kids throwing stones into a river. "Hey there, little friends!" he called out, "Do you know that the river is a home for fish and frogs?" The kids looked at each other, realizing that they didn't want to disturb their aquatic buddies. So, they decided to create a beautiful art project using leaves and pebbles instead. Nature loved it, and even the fish gave them a little splash of gratitude!

The stories of these magical saints remind us that kindness, laughter, and respect for nature are what make our world a happy place. As you explore the wonderful world of Zoroastrianism, remember to be like Asha, Vohu Manah, and Khordad. Let your imagination run wild, dance with your friends, and protect the animals and plants around you. After all, every little bit of love you share with nature makes it sparkle a little brighter!

Animal Adventures in Zoroastrian Land

Why Animals Are Our Friends

In Zoroastrianism, animals are like our furry and feathered friends who help keep the balance in nature. Imagine a world where animals throw dance parties in the forest, and every squirrel is a DJ spinning acorn tunes! Just think about how much fun it would be if cats could give you fashion advice and dogs had their own talk shows. Animals are not only cute and funny; they are important members of our planet's family. Zoroaster, the founder of Zoroastrianism, believed that we should treat animals with kindness and respect, just like we would want to be treated. After all, who wouldn't want a loyal dog or a wise old tortoise as a buddy?

Now, let's take a quick trip to the Zoroastrian creation story. Picture this: the world was all dark and quiet until Ahura Mazda, the wise creator, decided to throw a big party. He created everything from the sparkling stars to the buzzing bees, and guess what? He made animals too! Each creature was designed with a purpose, like a special ingredient in a cosmic recipe. The lion roars like a superstar, while the little ant carries tiny crumbs like a superhero. Every critter, from the mighty elephant to the tiniest worm, plays a role in keeping our planet healthy and happy. Isn't it cool how everyone has a job to do, just like in a team?

Speaking of teams, let's not forget the Zoroastrian festivals where animals get the spotlight! Imagine a big celebration where everyone dresses up as their favorite animal. You could see kids in fluffy bunny costumes hopping around while others pretend to fly like colorful birds. These festivals remind us to celebrate life and nature, showing our appreciation for all the creatures that share our world. So, next time there's a holiday, think about how you can honor animals. Maybe you can make a cake shaped like a cat or draw a picture of a dancing dolphin. The possibilities are endless!

Now, what about those key figures in Zoroastrianism? Zoroaster himself had a special relationship with animals. He was like the ultimate animal whisperer, understanding their needs and feelings. Imagine him sitting with a wise owl, discussing the mysteries of the universe! Zoroaster taught us that animals have their own spirits and deserve our love and protection. So whenever you see a puppy wagging its tail or a bird singing a sweet song, remember that they are trying to communicate with you. They might just be sharing secrets about how to be happy and kind!

Lastly, let's take a moment to think about how we can be guardians of animals. Zoroastrian values teach us to be kind and respectful, not just to our friends but to all living beings. If you see a spider spinning a web, don't be scared! Just think of it as a tiny artist creating a masterpiece. If you find a stray cat, maybe you could help it find a home. Every little act of kindness counts! So let's be the heroes of our own stories, protecting our animal friends and making the world a brighter, happier place for everyone. Remember, when we take care of animals, they take care of us too!

The Legend of the Sacred Cow

O nce upon a time, in the magical world of Zoroastrianism, there was a very special cow named Gava. Now, Gava wasn't your ordinary cow. She was a sacred cow, which meant she had a really important job in the universe. You see, Gava was responsible for nourishing the earth with her milk, and guess what? She was also a super-duper friend to all the plants and animals! Imagine a cow wearing a crown and a cape, flying around, helping all her buddies grow big and strong. That's Gava for you!

One sunny day, Gava decided to take a stroll through the fields. As she trotted along, she spotted a group of hungry little plants looking sad and droopy. "What's wrong, my leafy friends?" she asked, her voice as sweet as the freshest grass. The plants sighed,

"We're so thirsty! We need some water and sunshine!" Gava smiled and said, "Don't worry! I'll sprinkle my magical milk on you!" And with a light swish of her tail, she showered the plants with her creamy goodness. They perked up instantly, doing a happy dance in the breeze!

But while Gava was busy helping her plant pals, something mischievous was happening in the background. A cheeky little fox named Zorin thought it would be funny to play tricks on Gava. He snuck up and whispered, "Hey Gava, did you hear the news?

There's a giant cheese festival in the next field!" Gava's ears perked up, and she gasped, "Cheese? Oh, I love cheese!" But Zorin just chuckled and ran away, leaving Gava confused. "Is there really a cheese festival? Or is that just a silly fox tale?" she wondered.

Just then, a wise old owl named Ozzie swooped down and hooted, "Don't be fooled, dear Gava! Zorin loves to tease, but you know what's true? Your milk is far more precious than any cheese!" Gava thought for a moment and realized Ozzie was right. She had a special role to play, and that was to spread kindness and nourishment to everyone around her. So, with a big smile, she decided to host her own festival—a Milk and Kindness Festival! All the animals and plants were invited, and they would celebrate together, sharing laughter, joy, and of course, delicious milk!

And so, the legend of the Sacred Cow spread far and wide. Kids and animals all over the land learned that Gava's milk wasn't just tasty; it was a symbol of love and caring for nature. They discovered that every creature, big or small, played a part in making the world a happier place. Just like Gava, they learned to be guardians of the earth, sharing kindness and helping each other grow. And from that day on, whenever someone saw a cow, they would smile and remember the magical adventures of Gava, the sacred cow who taught everyone the true meaning of friendship and nature's wonders.

Protecting Our Furry and Feathered Friends

In the magical world of Zoroastrianism, our furry and feathered friends are not just cute and cuddly; they are superstars in the great show of life! Imagine if your pet cat could talk. What do you think it would say? Probably something like, "Feed me, human!" But in Zoroastrian belief, animals are more than just pets. They are part of the creation story, like the stars and the trees, helping to keep our planet balanced and happy. So, when you see a squirrel chasing its tail or a bird singing its heart out, remember that they are all part of a grand adventure created by Ahura Mazda, the wise spirit who made everything!

Now, let's talk about fire! You might be wondering, "What does fire have to do with our furry friends?" Well, in Zoroastrianism, fire is like a superhero—it keeps us warm, cooks our food, and lights up the dark. But here's the twist: fire also helps us care for animals! It reminds us to protect them and respect their homes. Imagine roasting marshmallows over a cozy campfire while a raccoon sneaks a peek at your tasty treats. That raccoon is hoping you'll share! Just like you wouldn't want to burn your marshmallows to a crisp, we should also avoid harming any creature that shares our planet.

Every year, Zoroastrians celebrate festivals that honor life and nature. Picture a giant picnic with animals invited! During these festivals, we sing, dance, and eat delicious food, all while remembering to appreciate the animals around us. It's like a birthday party, but instead of cake, we have gratitude! When you see a butterfly fluttering by, you can think of it as a little party guest, spreading joy and beauty. So, every time you celebrate, remember to give a little cheer for the animals that make our world a more fun place to live.

Let's not forget the amazing stories of Zoroaster and other saints! These stories are like bedtime tales, but instead of dragons and knights, they feature heroes who protect animals and nature. Zoroaster taught us to be kind, and what's kinder than sharing a snack with a hungry bird? Imagine leaving out some seeds for your feathered friends and watching them hop around like they just found a treasure! Every act of kindness, no matter how small, makes the world a happier place for both people and animals.

Lastly, Zoroastrian values guide us to treat all living beings with respect. Think of it like being a superhero for animals! When you see a stray dog, instead of running away, you can help by giving it some water or finding it a home. It's like being part of a secret club where everyone looks out for each other. So, as you begin your journey into the wonderful world of Zoroastrianism, remember that protecting our furry and feathered friends is a big part of being a true nature guardian. Together, we can make the world a better place, one wagging tail and chirping bird at a time!

The Great Beyond

Heaven and Hell

Exploring Heaven: The Land of Happy Souls

Welcome to the magical world of Heaven, the land where happy souls roam like playful puppies in a sunny park! In Zoroastrianism, Heaven is a special place filled with joy and laughter, where everyone is treated like a VIP. Imagine a giant candy store where the shelves are packed with endless sweets, and every bite brings a giggle! Here, the happy souls are busy having fun, sharing stories, and playing games that make even the most serious angels crack a smile.

Now, let's meet some of the coolest residents of Heaven! First up is the Great Creator, Ahura Mazda, who is like the ultimate game master. He keeps everything running smoothly and makes sure everyone is having the best time ever. Then there are the good spirits, known as the Yazatas, who are like the life coaches of the universe. They cheer everyone on, encouraging kindness and respect for nature. Picture them as fluffy guardians with wings, flapping around and spreading happiness like confetti at a birthday party!

But wait, there's more! In Heaven, every day is a festival. Imagine a place where it's always your favorite holiday! The skies sparkle with fireworks, and the air smells like freshly baked cookies. People gather to celebrate the wonders of nature, dancing and singing songs about trees, rivers, and friendly animals. And guess what? They even throw in a pie-eating contest just for fun! Heaven is a place where everyone can express their love for the Earth and share their gratitude for all the amazing things in life.

Of course, we can't forget about the animals! In Heaven, all creatures great and small are treated like royalty. The souls take care of their furry friends, making sure they're happy and well-fed. It's like a giant petting zoo where every animal gets a belly rub and a snack! The Zoroastrian belief

teaches us that protecting animals and nature is super important, and in Heaven, they take
that very seriously. So, if you ever
find a fluffy bunny or a curious squirrel, remember that they
have a special place in Heaven
too!

So, dear friends, as you embark
on your Zoroastrian adventure,
remember that Heaven is not just
a place up in the clouds. It's a
wonderful land filled with laughter, love, and the spirit of togeth-
erness. Think of it as the ultimate happy place where everyone is encouraged to be kind, re-

spectful, and protective of nature. And who knows? Maybe one day, you'll be part of that joyful crowd, sharing stories and giggles with all the happy souls!

The Not-So-Fun Place

Understanding Hell

In Zoroastrianism, there's a place that sounds totally un-fun, and that's Hell! Now, before you start imagining spooky ghosts and creepy crawlies, let's take a closer look at what this place is really about. Hell isn't just a fiery pit where you get chased by angry fire-breathing monsters; it's more like a time-out corner for those who forgot to be nice to others and didn't take care of the world around them. You know, like when you forget to feed your pet goldfish or leave your toys all over the place.

Imagine if you went to a really boring party where everyone is sitting around, mopey and grumpy, not having any fun at all. That's kind of what Hell is like in Zoroastrian beliefs. It's a place where people go when they don't follow the good path and make bad choices. In Zoroastrianism, we believe that being kind to others and caring for nature is super important. If someone chooses to be mean or doesn't help our planet, they might find themselves in this not-so-fun place, learning a lesson about how to be better next time!

But wait! Here's the good news: Hell isn't forever! Just like when you get sent to your room for not cleaning up after yourself, you can always come back and do better. In Zoroastrian stories, everyone has a chance to learn from their mistakes. So, if someone ends up in that boring party, they can figure out how to be nice and start taking care of the Earth. It's like having a second chance to win at a game after you've made a mistake.

Now, you might be wondering how we can avoid this not-so-fun place. The answer is simple: be kind and respectful! Treat animals well, help your friends, and re-member to recycle. Every little ac-tion counts. Zoroaster, the wise figure in our stories, teaches us that our choices matter. So, if you choose to be a hero for nature and your friends, you're on the right path to a much happier place—think of it as the ultimate fun zone, full of laughter and joy!

So, the next time you hear about Hell, remember it's just a big, boring timeout for those who forgot how to be kind. It's a reminder for all of us to cherish the world around us and the people in it. Let's be nature's guardians together, filled with fun and laughter, making sure that we never have to visit that dull place. After all, life is too short to spend in a boring party!

A Kid's Guide to Making Good Choices

Making good choices is like being a superhero for our planet! Zoroastrianism teaches us that every little decision we make can help protect the Earth, just like Zoroaster and his friends did in the olden days. Imagine you're in a comic book, and every time you choose to recycle or water a plant instead of ignoring it, you earn super points! So, let's grab our capes and dive into how we can make choices that are good for us, our furry friends, and the world around us.

First up, let's talk about the mighty power of recycling. It's like magic! When you put your empty juice box in the recycling bin instead of the trash, it transforms into something new. Maybe a shiny new park bench or even a spaceship for squirrels! Okay, maybe not a spaceship, but you get the idea. By recycling, you're helping reduce waste and making sure our animal pals have a clean place to live. So, the next time you finish a snack, think like Zoroaster and ask yourself, "What would a hero do?" Spoiler: A hero would definitely recycle!

Next, how about watering plants? Think of them as your green buddies who can't shout, "Hey, I'm thirsty!" When you water a plant, it's like giving it a big, refreshing drink at a fun party. Plants are super important because they help clean the air and provide homes for animals. So, the next time you see a wilting flower, channel your inner Zoroastrian and save the day with a watering can! You might even earn a few happy bees buzzing around to say thank you.

Now, let's get into the world of animals. In Zoroastrianism, animals are considered to be our friends, and it's our job to take care of them. If you see a stray cat or a dog looking for food, you can choose to help. Maybe you could leave out some food or tell an adult who can help them. When we treat animals with kindness, we create a world that's full of love and laughter. Plus, who wouldn't want a puppy as their sidekick?

Finally, let's sprinkle in some fun about festivals! Zoroastrian festivals are like giant birthday parties for nature and all the good things in life. During these celebrations, we can learn to share, respect, and appreciate everything around us. When you choose to join in the fun and help out, you're making a choice that brings joy to everyone, including the trees and flowers. So, dance, sing, and spread kindness like confetti at these celebrations.

Remember, every choice you make is like a small pebble in a pond, creating ripples that spread far and wide. By recycling, watering plants, helping animals, and celebrating with joy, you're not just making good choices; you're becoming a true guardian of nature, just like Zoroaster! So, put on your superhero cape and start making choices that are good for you, your friends, and our beautiful planet.

Zoroastrian Values

Kindness is Cool!

Being Nice to Nature: The Zoroastrian Way

Being nice to nature is like being friends with the coolest superhero ever! In Zoroastrianism, we believe that nature is not just a bunch of trees and animals; it's part of a big, magical family that includes us. Imagine if the trees could talk! They would probably tell you how much they love when you say, "Hello!" and give them a hug. Zoroastrian stories teach us that the Earth, sky, and all living things are gifts from Ahura Mazda, our wise and loving creator. So, when you step outside, remember that you're entering a magical playground where nature is waiting to be treated with kindness!

Now, let's talk about the little critters in our backyard. Did you know that Zoroastrians think all animals are super important?

They are like tiny superheroes, each with their special powers! For instance, the bee helps flowers bloom, and the squirrel keeps us entertained with its funny acrobatics. Zoroaster, the founder of Zoroastrianism, would probably give a thumbs-up to those who help animals. So, if you see a bird building its nest or a squirrel gathering acorns, cheer them on! It's like being their number one fan, and who doesn't love a good cheerleader?

Fire is another big deal in Zoroastrianism, and believe it or not, it has a personality too! Think of fire as the wise storyteller sitting around the campfire, sharing tales of our planet's adventures. Zoroastrians believe fire helps us remember to be nice to nature. When you see a flickering flame, you can think of all the warmth it brings, not just to us but to the plants and creatures too. So, if you ever roast marshmallows (yum!), remember to thank the fire for its magic. Just don't forget to be careful, or you might end up with more smoke than s'mores!

Festivals in Zoroastrianism are like the ultimate nature parties! We celebrate everything from the first day of spring to the harvest time when we gather to thank nature for being so awesome. Imagine a giant cake made of flowers, fruits, and vegetables! Everyone dances, sings, and plays games, reminding us of how much fun it is to be kind to the Earth. During these festivals, we can even make cards for our favorite plants and animals. Who wouldn't want to send a greeting card to a tree named Larry or a friendly rabbit named Ruby? It's all about spreading joy!

Lastly, being nice to nature is also about being kind to ourselves and each other. Zoroastrian values teach us to respect all living things. When we take care of the planet, we make it a happier place for everyone, including ourselves! So, next time you go outside, remember to smile at a flower, wave at a passing butterfly, or even pick up some litter (but only with grown-up help, of course!). By being nature's friends, we become superstars in Zoroastrianism, shining bright with kindness and respect for the world around us!

Sharing and Caring

Lessons from Zoroaster

Sharing and caring are like peanut butter and jelly – they just go together! Zoroaster, the wise leader of Zoroastrianism, taught us that being nice to each other and taking care of our planet is super important. Imagine if everyone in your class shared their toys and helped clean up the playground. Wouldn't it be a happier place? Zoroaster believed that when we share what we have, like yummy snacks or our favorite games, we make the world a brighter and more fun place for everyone.

Now, let's talk about caring for animals! In Zoroastrianism, animals are not just cute creatures we see at the zoo; they are our friends and part of our Earthly family. Zoroaster said that we should look after animals like they are our little brothers and sisters. So, if you see a sad puppy, don't just walk by! Give it a pat and maybe even share your lunch with it (but maybe not your broccoli). Taking care of our furry friends helps keep nature balanced and happy!

Fire is super important in Zoroastrianism, and it's not just for roasting marshmallows! Fire represents light, warmth, and the good spirit of sharing. When you see a fire, think of it as a symbol of friendship. Just like how we gather around a campfire to tell stories and laugh, Zoroastrians believe that fire brings people together. So, let's gather our friends and share stories about our favorite animals or adventures. The more we share, the brighter our fire of friendship glows!

Celebrating festivals is another way to show we care. Zoroastrian festivals are like the biggest birthday parties ever, but with more colorful decorations and delicious food! During these celebrations, families come together, share treats, and show gratitude for nature. Imagine a giant picnic where everyone brings their best dish! It's a time to appreciate the trees, rivers, and animals around us. So, when you go to a festival, remember to share not just food but also smiles and laughter. That's what makes the day special!

Lastly, Zoroaster taught us about kindness and respect. Just like superheroes, we can be guardians of our planet! When we pick up litter or help a friend, we show that we care. Being kind is like giving a high-five to the world. So, let's be the best buddies we can be, sharing our toys, caring for animals, and spreading kindness everywhere we go. Together, we can protect our beautiful Earth and make Zoroaster proud!

Respecting All Living Things

The Big Picture

Respecting all living things is like being the coolest super-hero of nature! Imagine if you had a magic power that made plants grow super tall and flowers bloom in all the colors of the rainbow. Well, in Zoroastrianism, we believe that every creature, big or small, has its own special role in the world. Whether it's a tiny ant marching in a line or a mighty elephant trumpeting in the wild, they all help keep our planet healthy and happy. So, the next time you see a spider in the corner of your room, remember that it's not just a creepy-crawly; it's a little guardian of the ecosystem!

Now, let's talk about our fiery friend, fire! In Zoroastrianism, fire is not just for roasting marshmallows (though that sounds delicious!). Fire represents truth and purity. It helps us remember to treat every living thing with respect, just like we keep our fires bright and shiny. If we think of fire as a cozy campfire, we should invite all nature's creatures to gather around it. Imagine a squirrel roasting a marshmallow or a bird telling stories! By respecting all living things, we keep our campfire blazing, creating a warm and friendly place for everyone.

Every year, we celebrate fun festivals that remind us how important nature is. One of the coolest festivals is called Nowruz, which means "new day!" During this time, we clean our homes, plant seeds, and even dance around like happy grasshoppers! It's a time to honor all the living things that share our world. When we sprinkle seeds in the ground, we're not just planting food; we're making a buffet for the birds and butterflies! And trust me, if you throw a party for nature, the bees will be buzzing with excitement, and the flowers will be dancing in the breeze.

Remember the great Zoroaster, our superhero of wisdom? He taught us that kindness and respect are like magic spells that can change the world! When he saw an animal in need, he didn't just walk by. He stopped, helped, and made sure all creatures felt loved. So, whenever you see a little critter or a lost kitten, think of Zoroaster. You can be a hero, too, by showing kindness and helping them out. Even the smallest act, like sharing your snack with a hungry bird, can create a ripple of goodness in nature.

In Zoroastrianism, we believe that when we treat every living thing with respect, we create a beautiful world where everyone can thrive. It's like being part of a giant family where everyone—plants, animals, and even humans—works together to make the Earth a happier place. So next time you see a butterfly fluttering by, give it a little wave and say, "You're awesome!" Because in the big picture of life, every little action counts, and together, we can be nature's greatest guardians!

An end to our Adventure

Ah, here we are—the end of our adventure in Once Upon a Time in Zoroastrianland! Don't worry, this isn't goodbye forever; it's more like a "See you later, alligator!" After all, adventures like these never really end—they just turn into stories we carry in our hearts (or scribble in the margins of our notebooks).

We've climbed whispering mountains, danced with cheeky flames, and probably giggled at least a hundred times at Angra Mainyu's grumpy attempts to ruin the party. But here's the thing about adventures: they always leave us with a little spark of something magical—a lesson, a memory, or maybe just a funny mental image of Ahura Mazda in superhero tights.

But before you run off to your next big quest (whether that's brushing your teeth or convincing your grown-ups to let you stay up 10 more minutes), let's remember the most important treasures we found here:

First, kindness is like a superpower—it doesn't need a cape or a fancy theme song. A little kindness goes a long way, whether it's helping a friend, caring for a pet, or even picking up a piece of litter. You might not have realized it, but every time you do something kind, Ahura Mazda probably gives you an invisible high-five.

Second, courage doesn't mean you're never afraid—it means you do the right thing even when you're afraid. Like standing up for a friend, trying something new, or being honest when it's hard. And honestly? That makes you pretty awesome.

And finally, remember that every day is a chance to be a hero. You don't need superpowers, magical swords, or talking animals (though, let's face it, that would be pretty cool). Sometimes, being a hero just means showing up, trying your best, and keeping your heart open to all the light and goodness the world has to offer.

So what's next, adventurer? Will you save a bug from a puddle? Plant a tree? Share your last cookie (gasp!) with a sibling? Whatever it is, remember—you're part of a story much bigger than yourself, and every good deed you do adds a little more light to the world.

As you close this book and head off to your next grand adventure, remember: Ahura Mazda believes in you, Angra Mainyu is probably still sulking in a corner somewhere, and the rivers, flames, and mountains are cheering you on.

Now, go out there, little hero. The world is waiting—and trust me, it's going to be epic. The end...or rather, the beginning of your next story!

Let's Meet
Psalm

Psalm Carnoustie is a passionate children's author dedicated to introducing young readers to the vibrant world of cultures, religions, and timeless wisdom from around the globe. With a warm and engaging storytelling style, Psalm crafts tales that spark curiosity, foster understanding, and celebrate diversity.

Believing that children are the seeds of a more compassion-ate future, Psalm is driven by the philosophy that early expo-sure to different beliefs and tra-ditions nurtures empathy, kind-ness, and open-mindedness. Her books serve as gentle guides, helping children see the beauty in differences while embracing the common threads that unite us all.

When she's not weaving enchant-ing stories, Psalm enjoys explor-ing cultural festivals, collecting folklore from faraway lands, and sharing moments of quiet reflec-tion in nature. Her stories are not just books—they are bridges, connecting little hearts to a world of understanding and acceptance.